Young Riders Guides

Buying and Keeping a Horse or Pony

The first book in the series, *Buying and Keeping a Horse or Pony* answers all the questions likely to be asked by the first-time pony-owner. First of all the authors describe the best ways of buying a suitable pony, for instance at a sale, through an advertisement, or from a friend. There is information on the different types and breeds of horse and pony, and lots of invaluable advice on such important matters as stabling, grazing, feeding, shelter, dangerous plants, 'tack' and the importance of cleanliness. At the end is an outline of the work of the Pony Club and a very useful glossary of horse terms.

Illustrated throughout with photographs and line drawings, this is an excellent introduction to the problems and delights of buying and caring for your own horse or pony.

Young Riders Guides

Buying and Keeping a Horse or Pony

Robert Owen and John Bullock

Beaver Books

First published in 1976 by
The Hamlyn Publishing Group Limited
London · New York · Sydney · Toronto
Astronaut House, Feltham, Middlesex, England

© Copyright Text Robert Owen/John Bullock 1976
© Copyright Line illustrations
The Hamlyn Publishing Group Limited 1976
ISBN 0 600 34503 3

Printed in England by
Hazell Watson & Viney Limited, Aylesbury, Bucks
Set in Linotron Univers Light
Line drawings by Gwen Green

Contents

Introduction

This book has been prepared in three parts: it gives basic information to help those who are considering buying a horse or pony; it deals with breeds and types; and it examines the problems which have to be faced when you have a horse or pony to look after.

But it is necessary to have more than money and a knowledge of caring for a horse or pony. Buying and keeping an animal, large or small, is a very big responsibility to take on. And you must recognise that responsibility before buying your first pony.

It may be that you will have had some previous experience of looking after a friend's pony, and this will be of value. Any experience will have shown you how complex is the routine which is demanded by a fit and happy pony.

If, however, you have had no previous experience, do not be disheartened. There is a vast amount to learn, and we hope you will find *Buying and Keeping a Horse or Pony* helpful and instructive.

Owning a pony, and being able to ride, should be fun. But *your* fun must always take second place.

R. O.
J. B.

Acknowledgements

The photographs in this book were supplied by the following:

British Spotted Horse and Pony Society: page 47
Equestrian (Press and General) Services Limited: pages 9, 14, 15, 56, 65, 70, 71 and photographs used on the cover
Clive Hiles; pages 44, 72
Irish Tourist Board: page 28
Leslie Lane AIIP: pages 30, 32, 36, 37, 38, 39, 41, 42, 43
Montague Lewis: page 34
Photonews: pages 20, 27, 46
Pony and Light Horse: pages 31, 35
Thomas A. Wilkie: page 10

Buying a horse or pony

How does one go about buying a horse or pony?
Let us examine four of the ways open to us when we set about the task of finding a suitable pony to buy: going to a horse sale, answering advertisements, buying through a horse dealer, or buying a pony already known to you.

These two animals, both well presented, show clearly the difference between a horse and pony.

Buying at a horse sale

In the British Isles and, indeed, throughout the world, the Horse Sale is the traditional place at which to buy and sell. Such sales are advertised, and may take place weekly on normal 'market' days, or they may be held occasionally at local cattle markets. In the

Interest is being shown at the ringside for this pony 'under offer'. The auctioneer is asking for bids, and the pony will shortly be changing ownership. This scene is typical of many rural horse sales; it is a scene repeated frequently in countries throughout the world.

specialist equestrian magazines and sometimes in the national press we can find a Horse Sale advertised to take place at a farm or riding establishment or even at a racecourse. And these sales will be conducted under the watchful eye of an experienced and qualified auctioneer.

A list or catalogue of the horses and ponies being offered for sale will be made available a few weeks before the given date. In the catalogue will be found the conditions of sale and the details of warranty and soundness of the stock being offered. It is a good idea to study these conditions most carefully. You will, of course, need a trailer or horse box to take home any horse or pony you buy. Or you might be able to arrange for a local contractor to do this for you.

Particular breeds of pony may be offered for sale during the autumn months. These sales usually take place in the region where the breed originated. The ponies being sold at these sales may have been brought in from running free, but most likely they will be from established breeders.

Buying through advertisements

We have found that one of the most satisfactory ways to buy is through answering one or other of the hundreds of advertisements which offer horses and ponies for sale in the equestrian press. In Great Britain, one of the best-known and authoritative of all equestrian journals is the weekly *Horse and Hound.*

Once having made contact with the seller, either by letter or by telephone, and having arranged a date on which it is convenient to meet, you can go with the assurance that on what you have heard the breed or type, height and age, colour and markings are what you are wanting, since all this will have been discussed before you leave your home. When you meet the seller, and see and judge the horse he has on offer, you can make your decision in leisurely and congenial surroundings.

The advertisements use a variety of different phrases – all of which you will need to understand if you feel any is worth following up and the journey you will have to make to see what is being offered is to be worthwhile.

Some ponies are advertised as being 'bomb-proof'! And that can mean almost anything! It might indicate that the pony is so docile it is hardly a ride; or it might mean the owners have had it for a long time and, having got used to them and their ways, the pony *appears* to do nothing wrong. But, beware! Being bomb-proof does not mean the pony will never bolt or become excited.

11

From the pages of *Horse and Hound*

Horses are frequently advertised as being 'not a novice ride'. This can sometimes be read as a horse that is a somewhat difficult proposition, and is not for the inexperienced. Certainly not for someone buying for the first time! Neither will this type of horse be likely to give much peace of mind to the parent or to the rider.

But having said this, most advertisements do give a clear and honest indication of the horse or pony being offered. Do find out all you can before you set off to see the animal; make your judgement; see the horse or pony being ridden, and then ride it yourself. And, always insist that your veterinary surgeon must carry out an examination before you will finally buy.

Buying through a dealer

A horse dealer makes his living by being able to find what his customers require. Very, very few dealers live up to the bad reputation which has been given them in various books and films. If you really know exactly what you require you can go to a horse dealer. But the pleasure of being able to see and select will not then be yours. No dealer will ever insist you buy what he has found for you — especially if it is not all that you had hoped for.

Buying a pony known to you

This might have been headed 'Buying from a friend', though that would not be exactly what we mean! Ponies come on to the market for several reasons, one of which is that the rider has outgrown the mount. In this case owners love to know just who will be buying, and if you are known to them, so much the better. Perhaps a pony, well known to you at local shows, is one that you will have ridden — especially if it is owned by a friend. You will know something about it, something of how it performs, and quite a lot about its temperament — all valid reasons to take into account.

Knowledgeable friends and other people such as the District Commissioner of your local Branch of the Pony Club will always be available to give their help and guidance.

What is a pony?

Years ago people talked of ponies as being simply small horses. But this is not how we think today. Throughout the world the several different breeds of pony are recognised as being peculiar to a special location or a region, or to the part of the world in which that particular breed thrives.

It is as a result of selective breeding and the protection of certain characteristics that ponies today can be seen as part of the one species, *Equus caballus*, meaning the immediate forerunner of the modern horse.

The official definition of a pony is that it is a horse not standing over 14·2 hands. This will show how complicated it is when we try in a few words to make clear the differences between a pony and a horse!

On pages 30–43 details are given of the nine British native ponies. Today, the Breed Societies, the bodies which do so much to maintain the true characteristics of the breed, register pure-bred ponies in the Stud Books and Supplementary Registers. Other bodies, such as the National Pony Society, Ponies of Britain and the British Show Pony Society, set the standards by which the various breeds are judged.

The Shetland is one of the smallest of pony breeds.

This most suitable and lovely pony has won two rosettes for its young riders. It has been placed in both a First Ridden Pony event and in a Leading Rein class.

What must be considered before buying a pony?

This is a most difficult question to answer, since there are so many factors which must come into the reckoning. For example, you will face a different series of problems if you are keeping a pony in the middle of a town, from someone who is keeping a pony in the country. Test yourself – see if you can give a 'yes' to the following:

1   Have you had some experience in looking after a pony?
2   Have you helped at a riding school? Or looked after a pony belonging to a friend?
3   Do you understand the responsibility you take on once you have a pony of your own?
4   Have you learned to ride well?
5   Have you joined the Pony Club or other riding organisation?
6   Are you sure you have the use of sufficient grazing land? And is this land really suitable for a pony?
7   Do you know what is meant by 'supplementary feeding'?
8   Are you prepared to read and learn all you can about keeping ponies; to take advice from those who have experience; and to spend each day the time which is so necessary to see that your pony, whether grass-kept or stable-kept, is well cared for?

Is there a rough guide to help find the right size of pony?

Certainly, there can be no firm and sure guide! Young people vary in height and weight, and to lay down a hard and fast rule that someone who is eight years old should 'fit' a 12·2 hands pony would be ridiculous. In any case, it would also depend on whether or not the eight-year-old had any experience of riding, and what was being asked of the pony.

On page 26 we show how ponies are measured and, provided a young person is of average height and build, the following would be a *very rough* guide:

height of pony	approximate age of rider
under 11 hands	under 7 years
between 11 and 12·2 hands	between 7 and 9 years
between 12·2 and 13·2 hands	between 9 and 12 years
between 13·2 and 14·2 hands	between 12 and 14 years
between 14·2 and 15·2 hands	between 14 and 16 years

If you look at the two ponies and riders pictured on the left you can see clearly that one pony is much too small for its rider and the other is too big. The pony and rider on this page are well matched.

What are the points of a horse?

One of the first things you must learn are the names and positions given to the 'points' of a horse or pony. Unless these are recognised by you it will be difficult to discuss many aspects of equestrianism or to follow the information to be found in books of instruction. The points will also be used when deciding on what you should be looking for when choosing a horse or pony, and when talking with your veterinary surgeon.

But, even when you know the names of all the points, you will still find there is much to learn!

The points shown on the facing page are some of those you will most frequently use. More advanced books and manuals will give longer lists.

1	Ear
2	Forelock
3	Forehead
4	Eye
5	Cheekbone
6	Lower jaw
7	Nostril
8	Muzzle
9	Upper lip
10	Lower lip
11	Chin groove
12	Bars of jaw
13	Cheek
14	Gullet
15	Trachea (windpipe)
16	Point of shoulder
17	Breast
18	Pectoral muscle
19	Forearm
20	Elbow
21	Knee
22	Cannon bone
23	Fetlock joint
24	Pastern
25	Tendons
26	Girth
27	Base of neck
28	Belly
29	Sheath
30	Stifle
31	Shin
32	Chestnut
33	Coronet
34	Hoof (wall of foot)
35	Heel
36	Ergot
37	Fetlock
38	Hock
39	Point of hock
40	Gaskin
41	Tail
42	Buttocks
43	Dock
44	Hip joint
45	Thigh
46	Quarter
47	Croup
48	Point of croup
49	Back
50	Withers
51	Mane
52	Crest
53	Poll

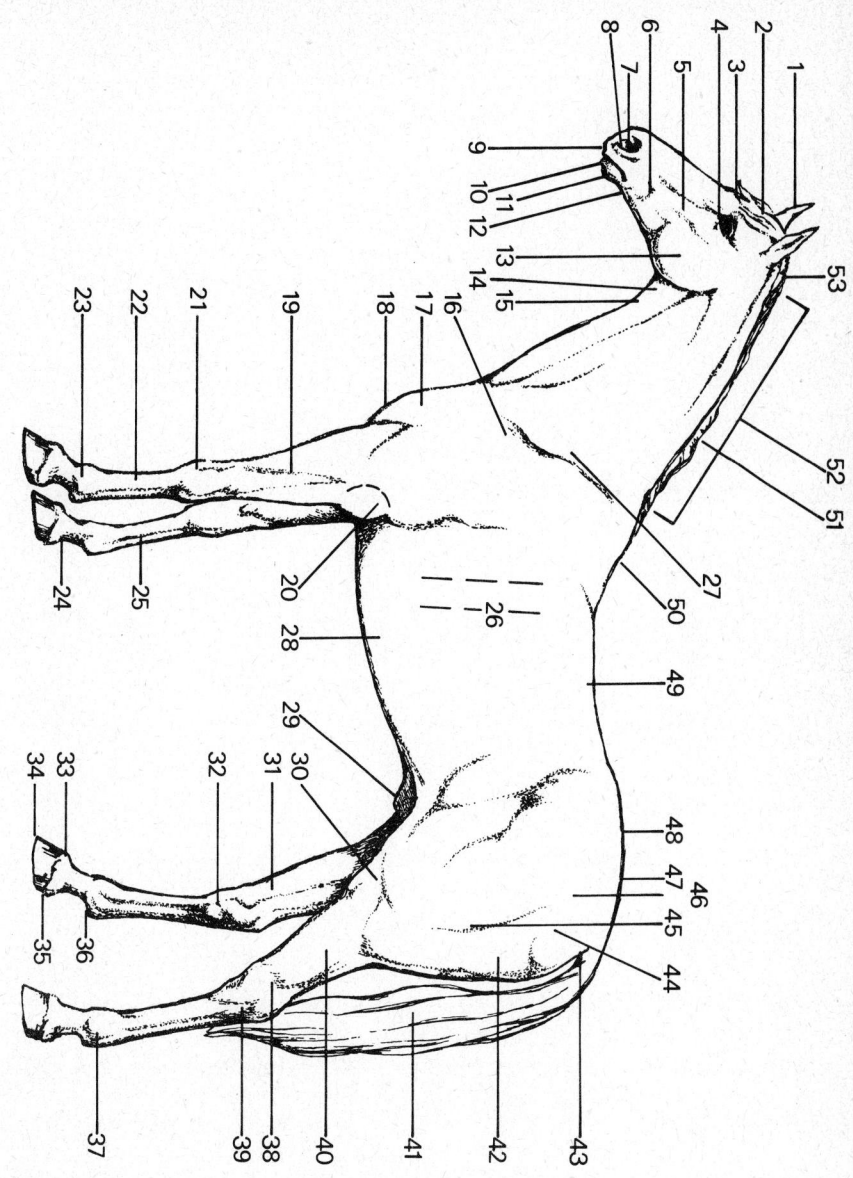

19

Haroun, owned by the Tollard Park Arabian Stud, who was male Champion Arab in England in 1974.

What is conformation?

This word is constantly used when discussing horses and ponies. It means, in very simple terms, the way the animal is 'put together'. Dictionaries tell us that the word conformation means form or shape – and that is a very good definition for our purposes.

A horse or pony with *good* conformation is well put together and of pleasing overall proportions. Even to an unskilled eye it is not difficult to recognise a horse with good conformation: the head, with clear and well-set eyes and neck, should neither be too large nor too small, and should be set on to good shoulders; the back must be straight, ending with strong hindquarters; the ribs and girth should be wide and large enough to house good lungs, and the legs firm and straight.

Look closely at the Arab horse in the photograph above. This picture shows good conformation. Now compare this with the drawing opposite. Here we have asked our artist to draw the sort of horse you *must* avoid – here is nothing but bad conformation!

Since when beginning we can never get our ideal, we should be satisfied if the horse or pony we would like to buy has some measure of good conformation. But always avoid buying a badly 'put together' animal.

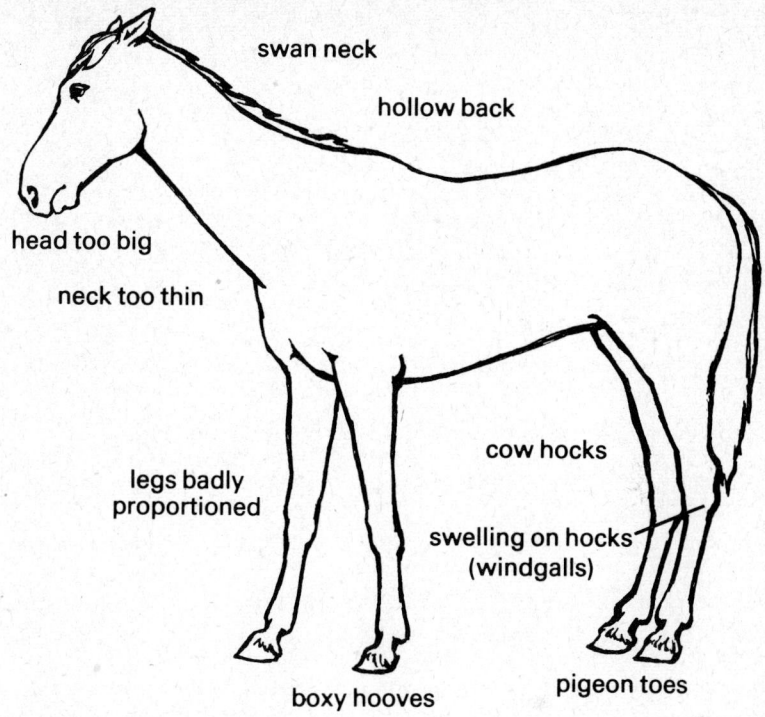

swan neck

hollow back

head too big

neck too thin

cow hocks

legs badly
proportioned

swelling on hocks
(windgalls)

boxy hooves

pigeon toes

Points of conformation

Head   Must be in good proportion to the overall look of the horse or pony. The bone structure should be well defined.

Eyes   Should be kind, prominent and widely set.

Ears   Should be set wide and forward and show alertness.

Neck   Neither too long nor too short and set well into shoulders.

Shoulders   Sloping in a line from the withers to the point of the shoulder.

Back   Must blend with front and hindquarters. A short back is considered best, but this must show good proportions overall.

Hindquarters   Clean and muscular.

Legs   Square and solid in stance. Forelegs when seen from the front to be straight. Viewed from behind the legs must be straight and perpendicular to the body. There must be no puffy joints.

Pasterns   Neither too large nor too short.

Hoofs   Rounded and 'clean'.

What should one look out for when trying a pony?

When you see a likely pony, there are several things to watch out for:

1   If the pony is not in the field when you arrive, why not? Maybe it is difficult to catch.

2   Can a child put the saddle and bridle on unaided, and mount unaided either from the ground or a bank or bale of straw? If the pony won't stay still and allow a child to deal with it itself, you are buying yourself a full-time job.

3   Will the pony do as it is asked in its home surroundings without trying to dodge out of it and get back to its friends or own stable? If it tries to assert its own will this is known as being 'nappy', a most undesirable characteristic for a child's pony.

4   Is it really foolproof with traffic, especially big lorries? To buy a pony nowadays which is not 100% reliable with traffic is madness, and you will never have a moment's peace of mind if you do.

5   Does it look animated and happy, with ears pricked, or are the ears back showing signs of a nasty temperament? A bad or nervy temperament can never be wholly cured, especially by a child, because another child has probably caused it, through ignorance, in the first place.

6   No doubt you will have been told the age, but it is as well to be able to check this for yourself. A horse's age is shown by its teeth, and if you study the drawings on page 25, you should be able to get some idea for yourself. After the age of seven or eight a horse is said to be 'aged', and then the development of the teeth may vary, and the exact age is difficult to determine.

7   Will the pony walk quietly and willingly into a horse box or trailer? This is known as 'quiet to box'. If not, you may well let yourself in for a lot of frustration and trouble because probably before long you will want to move somewhere beyond hacking distance.

(Reprinted by kind permission from *Keeping a Pony* by Jane and Melinda St Clair)

What is a 'vet's certificate'?

Before buying a horse or pony it is most strongly recommended that you first obtain your own veterinary surgeon's report. And *always* go by what he says! Even the most experienced of horsemen will never consider paying for a horse or pony until an examination has been undertaken, and until the report shows the animal is satisfactory. A vet's certificate will also be necessary if you approach an insurance company for insurance cover against the animal's illness, accident or death.

A vet's certificate will, if the animal is sound, give the correctly measured height, the age of the horse or pony, and something to the effect that an examination has been satisfactorily carried out, and that the horse or pony is sound, as far as the vet can judge, in wind and limb. A more advanced examination can be given, when the vet will use X-rays and other medical aids.

The examination given by a veterinary surgeon will cover the breathing and lung action of a horse, the heart and pulse rate, both when quiet and after having been galloped, an investigation of the eyes and a general examination of the head, a close look at the legs to check for splints, etc., and a check of the feet. He will also want to check the horse's action at the walk, trot and canter (see below).

How does one tell the age of a pony?

A pony's age is found by looking closely at his teeth. Different marks and shapes occur on the teeth at varying ages, though when a horse or pony reaches the age of eight years it becomes more difficult to be absolutely certain of age.

To examine the teeth first open the pony's mouth. To do this you use both hands, one for the upper lip and one for the lower. Do not hold too tightly on to the pony's jaw, but gently put your thumb and forefinger on to the bars of his lower jaw between the incisor teeth and molars (see the illustrations below).

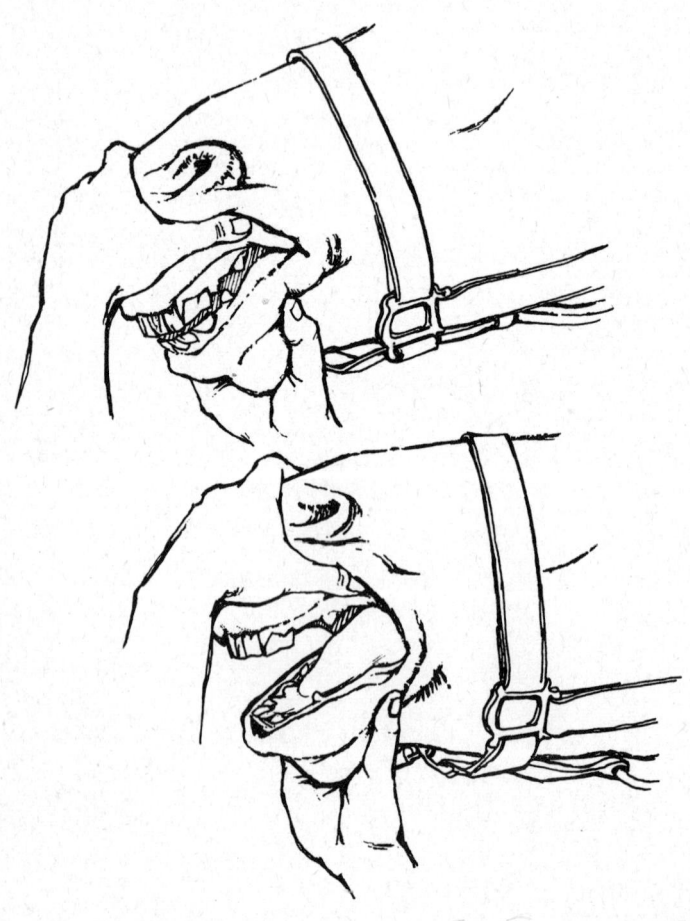

Birth to 6 months: The temporary incisors or milk teeth begin to appear after 10 days.

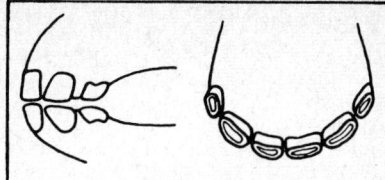

2 years: There is now a full set of milk teeth, showing small dark rings on the biting edges.

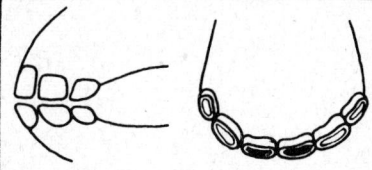

3 years: First permanent teeth. At first they show no marks, but these soon appear.

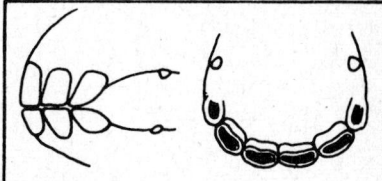

5 years: A 'full mouth' of permanent teeth. Corner incisors meet only at the front.

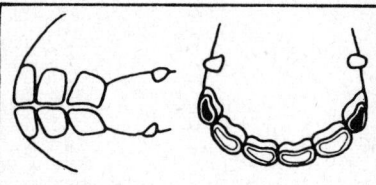

7 years: Corner incisors now meet, and a small hook appears on the upper corner incisors.

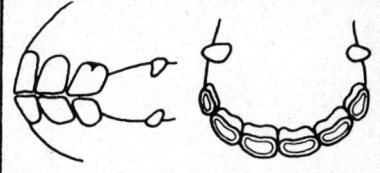

9 years: 'Galvayne's Groove' appears at top corner incisors. At this age it is about 3 mm (1/8 inch) long.

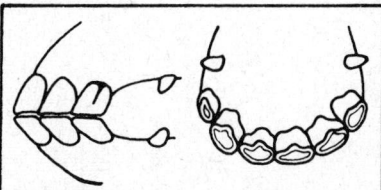

15 years: Teeth have become more triangular and are beginning to slope out.

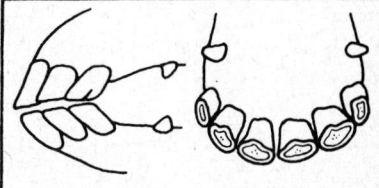

25 years: Slope of incisors is very pronounced. Galvayne's Groove is disappearing.

How are ponies measured?

The height of a pony is the measurement found when taking the line from the ground to the highest part of the withers. In English-speaking countries measurement is given in hands and inches, each hand being 4 inches (10 cm). This somewhat peculiar and, in the early days, not very accurate measure came from what was thought to be the width of an average man's hand.

Other countries today give and record height measurements only in metres and centimetres.

The main characteristics of many breeds are determined by height, and the height of a pony will also determine into which class or event it may compete or be shown at a horse show. Therefore it becomes increasingly important to have some accurate record of the height of a pony.

The true measurement is taken when a pony is standing on level ground; allow 1·25 cm (¹/₂ inch) for the shoe if the pony is shod.

Breeds

What are mountain and moorland ponies?

These are the breeds which are known as 'British Native Ponies'. The nine types can be grouped into three regional sections: the northern group, comprising the Highland, Dales and Fell; the western group, comprising the Welsh and the Connemara from Ireland; the southern group, comprising the Dartmoor, Exmoor and New Forest. By itself, though very much part of the northern group, is the Shetland – the smallest of all the mountain and moorland ponies.

Each of the native breeds has inherited wonderful qualities. They are ideal for living out at grass, they are extremely hardy, and they make excellent riding ponies and ponies from which to breed. Competitions are held at many shows throughout the world which seek best of breed. A description and photograph of each of the British native breeds are given on the following pages.

Connemara ponies in their natural environment

In addition to the British native pony breeds we shall be discussing in the next few pages, there are several breeds which are equally well-known in their own countries. These include the Fjord, Icelandic, Falabella, Barthais, Dulmen and the different breeds in Australia, New Zealand and elsewhere.

1 Highland
2 Dales
3 Fell
4 Welsh
5 Connemara
6 Dartmoor
7 New Forest
8 Exmoor
9 Shetland

The Highland pony

The Highland is one of the largest and strongest of the native pony breeds and is found in the highlands of Scotland and in some of the outer islands. There are two main types: those who live and thrive on the mainland and who stand between 13·2 hands and 14·2 hands; and those found on the islands – a smaller breed standing between 12·2 hands and 13·2 hands. The larger breed are sometimes referred to as 'Mainland' ponies.

These are ideal as riding ponies and are used extensively for trekking and hill climbing.

A certain amount of foreign blood has been introduced, much of which is Arab, and the Highland is also a good, honest working pony used for carrying loads for the crofters. They are extremely healthy and strong, surviving throughout the year on some of the toughest country and in the severest of weather conditions.

Description *Height* Between 13·2 hands and 14·2 hands *Colours* Black, brown with occasional dun and grey. No white markings

Head Well carried, attractive *Ears* Short and well set *Neck* Strong and not over-pronounced *Back, loins and quarters* Short back with a slight curve. Powerful quarters and loins *Tail* Strong and well set on, carried gaily, with a plentiful covering of hair almost reaching the ground
Breed Society The Highland Pony Society

The Dales pony
Like the Fells, the Dales are natives of the northern part of England. For centuries they have lived between the Pennine Chain of hills to the west and the coastline of Durham and Yorkshire to the east. Another similarity to the Fells is that they also were used to carry lead from the mining areas to the ports along the north-east coast.

The Dales are generally larger than the Fell ponies, usually standing well up to 14·2 hands. They are the heaviest and perhaps strongest of all the British native breeds. The breed has immense stamina and always has good legs and feet.

Today the Dales are found mainly in Durham, Northumberland and parts of Yorkshire and, although appearing more frequently in the show rings, the breed is ideal for the growing demand for ponies suitable for trekking and trail riding. They are quiet and gentle and are able to carry a full-grown person all day in the fells. In fact, it is claimed that the Dales, once broken, are capable of doing all the work required on a small farm.

Description *Colours* Many are black, though there are bays, browns and greys *Head* A neat head, well balanced with the overall conformation of the breed *Ears* Small and neatly set *Back, loins and quarters* Strong and full *Tail* Modest and carried rather low *Feet* Good feet and well feathered heels
Breed Society The Dales Pony Society

Fell pony

The Fell pony

The Fell pony is a breed peculiar to Cumbria, formerly comprising the counties of Cumberland and Westmorland. This area, bordering on the Lake District, is in the north-west corner of England, its eastern flank being the Pennines which run from north to south for a distance of nearly 300 miles.

The Fell is a strong and powerfully built pony, used in the seventeenth, eighteenth and early nineteenth centuries to carry heavy loads of lead from the mines to the ports on the north-eastern coastline. These heavy loads were taken on routes over the Pennines and across the bleakness of Westmorland and Durham. Many of the pack trails still remain.

As with all the British native breeds, the Fell pony is an excellent riding pony, standing usually about 13·2 hands. The breed has been developed into a highly-prized show pony, though when seen in its natural habitats it sometimes appears wild and rough. The Fell is good breeding stock and makes an ideal pony for trekking.

Description *Height* Up to 13·2 hands *Colours* Mostly entirely black, but some bays, browns or greys are seen *Head* This is small and well set on, with a broad forehead *Ears* Well formed and small *Neck* Strong, but not too heavy *Back, loins and quarters* A muscular body with strong and generous quarters. Powerful loins *Feet* Well shaped and tough on long and clean hocks *Tail* Well set and highly carried
Breed Society The Fell Pony Society

The Welsh pony

Accepted throughout the world as being among the most beautiful of all pony breeds, the Welsh also have superb qualities as children's riding ponies. Many, when thinking of the Welsh breeds, which are split into four sections, consider them as show ponies, seldom giving thought to the many types of other breeds which carry Welsh blood and which perform so well when jumping, eventing or hunting. The Welsh Stud Book caters for each of the separate sections which for many hundreds of years have lived and roamed on the Welsh mountains. They have developed a wonderful disposition and are intelligent, courageous and honest. The Sections shown in the Stud Book are quite distinctive and each has been given a detailed official description. No Welsh pony can be piebald or skewbald — all other colours are recognised.

These colts are typical Welsh mountain ponies.

The Welsh mountain pony (Section A)
A most beautiful pony whose height does not exceed 12 hands. It is sure-footed, sound and has the kindest of temperaments. Section A ponies have good movement and balance and are very safe in the hands of small children. They are natural jumpers and unequalled in the show ring. All Sections of the Stud Book are descended from the mountain pony and have these qualities.

Section A

The Welsh pony (Section B)
Larger than the pony in Section A, the Welsh pony stands at a height not above 13·2 hands. This breed is still used to carry a man shepherding and hunting in the hills of Wales. It is much in demand as a child's second pony, having all the qualities of the modern riding pony while retaining the type, character and hardiness of the native pony.

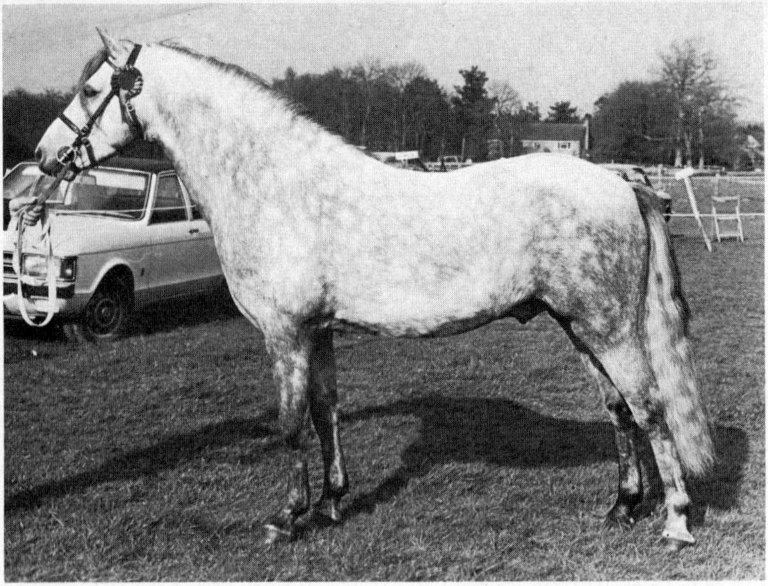

The Welsh pony or cob type (Section C)

The height must not exceed 13·2 hands. This is a very sure-footed pony who is capable of carrying either a full-grown man or a child. Used widely for hunting, trekking and in harness.

The Welsh cob (Section D)

A strong and active sort, useful for both riding and driving. Standing up to nearly 15·3 hands, the average Welsh cob is a little above the height of a pony. This particular breed is now one of the best of the smaller horses.

Breed Society (for all Sections) The Welsh Pony and Cob Society

Top left: Section B
Bottom left: Section C
Below: Section D

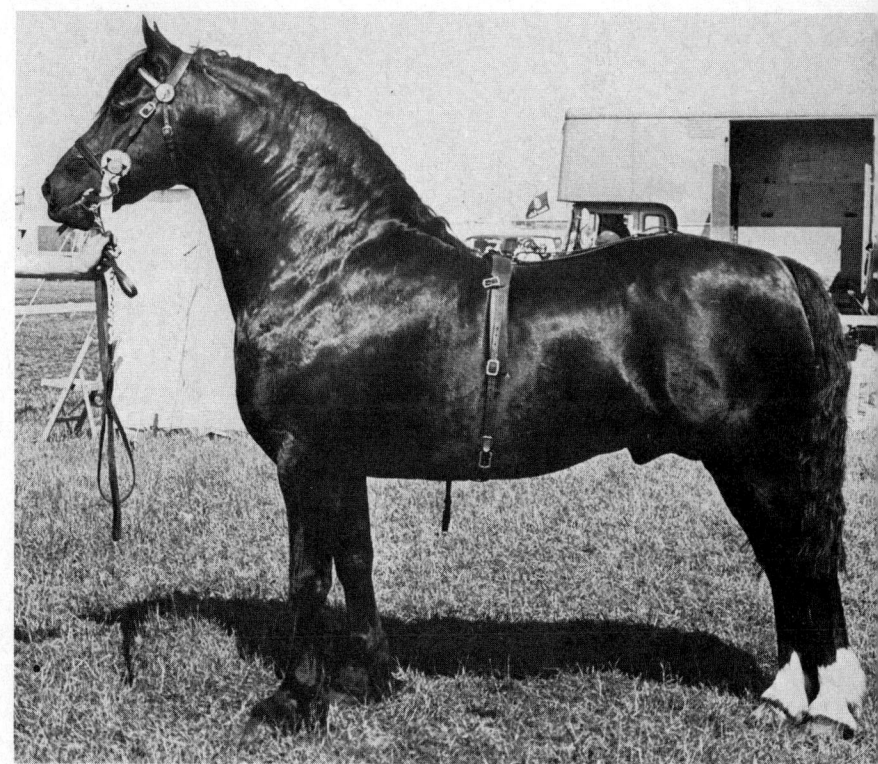

The Connemara pony

There is but one native breed of pony in Ireland, the Connemara. In the west of Ireland, near to the wild Atlantic Ocean, lies the district of Connemara, from which the breed has been named. This is a particularly rugged part of the country with a mixture of rocky ground, mountainous slopes, lakes and bogs – the ideal place to permit a hardy and intelligent pony to breed and thrive. Apart from a few of the more fertile valleys, the grazing is sparse and poor. And this has gone to make the Connemara a most hardy type of pony, well suited to life in the toughest of conditions.

As with so many mountain and moorland breeds, the Connemara has been crossed very successfully with Thoroughbred stock. This has produced a number of well-known internationally famous jumpers. But the pure-bred Connemara has a great variety of uses. It is valuable as a farm animal; it has a natural ability to jump; it is sure-footed and gentle in its approach, and yet it is bold and honest in its use in all forms of equestrian sport.

Standing just under 14 hands, the Connemara shows up well when judged alongside British native bred ponies.

Description (taken from the Stud Book) *Colour* Grey, black, bay, brown, dun, with occasional roans and chestnuts *Head* Well balanced head and neck *Body* Compact, deep, standing on short legs *Bone* Clean, hard, flat, measuring 7 to 8 inches (18 to 20 cm) below the knee *Action* Free, easy and true movement
Breed Society The Connemara Pony Society

The Dartmoor pony

The Dartmoor pony has from earliest times lived and roamed in a rugged part of south-west England. The area, swept in the winter months by high winds and severe gales, offers little in the way of feeding. Protection from the climate is found in and around the high tors and well-wooded lower slopes, but the moor is rock

strewn and only a very hardy and sure-footed pony would have survived. The Dartmoor is a great favourite as a children's riding pony, and is excellent foundation stock for the breeding of larger ponies. Standing at a maximum height of 12·2 hands, the Dartmoor offers practically everything one could look for in a pony – it is good looking, honest and gentle. With its hardy background and nature it makes an ideal pony to live out at grass.

Description *Height* Not exceeding 12·2 hands *Colours* Bay, black or brown preferred, but no colour bar except skewbald and piebald *Head* Small and breedy and well set *Ears* Small and alert *Neck* Not too long or too short. It should be strong, but not heavy *Back, loins and quarters* Strong and covered with muscle *Feet* Tough and well-shaped *Tail* Set high and quite full
Breed Society The Dartmoor Pony Society

The New Forest pony

The New Forest, which is in Hampshire, has many square miles of woodland, heath and marshy bogs. Today there are few parts which can be called true forest, and many of the native ponies, who have lived in the district since earliest times, run loose and live near to the roads which take thousands of holiday-makers in their cars towards the south-coast resorts and holiday centres in the south-west.

New Forest ponies are popular throughout the world, especially in Europe, and thrive in a variety of conditions. When cross-bred they produce excellent small hunters and make one of the best-tempered, kindly and gentle of riding ponies.

Standing between 12·2 hands and 14·2 hands, New Forest ponies, which can be any colour except piebald or skewbald, are up to any of the larger native breeds. For many years they were used extensively for general work on farms and small-holdings. They were also in demand as pack ponies, carrying quite heavy loads over long distances. With the introduction of blood from other breeds – both Arab and Thoroughbred – they are recognised as one of the best all-round ponies in the world.

Description *Height* Varies from 12 hands to 14·2 hands *Colours* Any colour except piebald and skewbald *Head* Well set on *Back, loins and quarters* Short with good strong loins and quarters.
Breed Society New Forest Pony Breeding and Cattle Society

New Forest pony

The Exmoor pony

On the wild and lonely moors, part of which are in Devon and part in Somerset, lives the oldest of the native pony breeds – the Exmoor. This is a sturdy, agile pony, though there are today few places on the moors where the pure-bred ponies live.

Like the Dartmoor, the Exmoor makes an excellent riding pony for children in spite of its small size. The true-bred Exmoor does not make more than 12·2 hands, though some of the stallions are found at 12·3 hands. Those that still live on the moors find little sustenance in the moorland grass – yet they thrive there, just as they have done since earliest times.

The Exmoor also makes a most useful hunter; it is safe-footed and highly intelligent. It is also most adaptable when put across severe courses in cross-country and other events.

Description *Height* Up to 12·3 hands for stallions; to 12·2 hands for mares *Colours* Bay, brown or dun, but no white markings anywhere. The muzzle and flanks are mealy *Head* Rather long with a deep-set jaw *Ears* Short and thick with a mealy colour inside *Neck* Arched *Back, loins and quarters* The back is strong, and the chest is deep and wide *Feet* Neat and firm on short and clean legs **Breed Society** The Exmoor Pony Society

Exmoor pony

The Shetland pony

The Shetland is the smallest of the British native ponies. It has been proved that it has maintained its small stature in its native Shetland Islands for over 2000 years. The extreme hardiness of the Shetland has enabled it to thrive under very adverse grazing and weather conditions, but it will enjoy life in any climate. If pure bred it will not become over-height. Shetlands, if they are Registered, must not stand above 40 inches (1·01 metres) at three years and under, and not more than 42 inches (1·06 metres) at four years and over.

Ideally, Shetland ponies thrive best on a large run of rough grazing, but, under proper management and conditions, they can well be kept in small fields and paddocks. Fresh water must always be available and hay is invariably essential to supplement the grass during winter months for all ponies.

Description *Colours* Any colour known in horses *Head* Small with a wide forehead. The muzzle must be broad *Ears* Neat and small and well-placed *Neck* Long, well arched and ending in a well defined wither *Back, loins and quarters* The body and loins must be strong and muscular, the quarters broad and long *Feet* Round, open and very hard *Tail* Long and straight and set high
Breed Society The Shetland Pony Stud Book Society

43

Douglas Bunn's magnificent Heavyweight Hunter, Selsey Bill, 16·3 hands and seven years of age. He has won many first prizes and Championships at major shows throughout the British Isles.

What are the breeds of horses?

The space available permits us to deal only briefly with horse breeds and breeding. We will look at the Arab and Thoroughbred, and would advise those who wish to know more about this vast subject to consult some of the many specialist books which are available.

Whether our intention is to buy a horse solely for hacking or hunting, or whether the horse we are looking for is to be used for showing, we are set with the problem we will face when seeking a horse for jumping – we have to find him! There is always a number of good quality horses for sale. And some not so good! Our difficulty comes in making a final decision, and making the right choice of breed or type.

The Arab

The Arab has had the greatest influence of all on the world's horse population. In practically every type, from the Thoroughbred to the heavy working horses, from show ponies to show hunters, we find strains of Arab blood. The Arab is a most beautiful animal, as the picture on page 20 shows. It can be traced back for more than 5000 years.

Standing usually between 14·0 hands and 15·3 hands the Arab is not a big horse. It is renowned for its soundness, staying power and ability to carry weights which seem out of proportion to its size. It lives well in most climates, from desert wastes to the more lush grasslands of the northern and southern hemispheres.

Pure-bred Arabs are registered in the various stud books which are kept by the Arab Horse societies.

Captain Elwyn Hartley Edwards has written: 'All horses in competitive sport derive from the Arab to some extent and as a pure-bred he is supreme in the long distance endurance rides, though in his pure form he plays hardly any part in show-jumping or three-day events. Arab blood, outside strictly Thoroughbred breeding, continues to play a vital part in the development and upgrading of other breeds.' (*The Complete Book of the Horse* published by Ward Lock, London)

The *Anglo-Arab*, now popular in showing classes, show-jumping, eventing and other fields of equestrian sport, is the result of the cross of Arab and Thoroughbred. This, to many people, is the perfect saddle horse. Bigger than the pure-bred Arab, it stands between 15 hands and 16·3 hands.

The Thoroughbred

The modern Thoroughbred traces its ancestry back to three Arabian stallions which were brought to England during the latter part of the seventeenth century and the early part of the eighteenth century. These were the Byerley Turk, the Darley Arabian and the Godolphin Arabian.

Today, the Thoroughbred will still show traces of his Arabian beginnings and the breed has had enormous influence on many breeds throughout the world. Many show ponies are a cross of their native breed with part Arab or Thoroughbred.

With its long, easy action, and great turn of speed, the Thoroughbred is today principally found in the world of horse racing. Usually standing between 15·3 hands and 17 hands, it makes an excellent riding horse, with superb conformation.

A good all-round horse suitable for all types of equestrian activities. The horse and rider, both well turned-out, are ready to compete in a Riding class.

Right: A British Spotted pony, which is similar to the Appaloosa.

Though frequently excitable and difficult to manage in show-jumping and dressage competitions, the Thoroughbred is perhaps the ideal cross, often being mated with half-bred mares or with Arab or Anglo-Arab crosses.

Other horses

Not all horses are bred from Arab or Thoroughbred stock. The ancestors of many successful show jumpers and eventers cannot be traced. Perhaps all too frequently breeding and cross-breeding is haphazard. In many cases owners may know something about the sire of their horse, but will look blank when asked about the dam. This does not necessarily take away from them the confidence and pleasure they get from owning a horse. Some are lucky enough to own a pure-bred, others would not change their part-bred for anything in the world.

Among some of the well-known breeds from the world of horses are: Andalusian (Spain); Ardennais (France and parts of Western Europe); Appaloosa (United States); Breton (France); Cleveland Bay (Great Britain); Haflinger (Austria); Hanoverian (Germany); Holstein (Germany); Irish Draught (Ireland); Lipizzaner (Austria); Morgan (United States); Pahlavan (Iran); Palomino (United States); Percheron (France); Quarter Horse (United States); Shire (Great Britain); Waler (Australia).

By what colours are horses and ponies known?

As a general rule the following show the recognised colourings:

Black   A black body with black mane and tail.

Brown   Dark brown colouring overall, with brown mane and tail.

Bay   Brown body with black mane and tail and black points, i.e., the muzzle, tips of ears and the lower part of the limbs.

Chestnut   A reddish-brown body with mane and tail of similar colouring. Variations of the chestnut are the 'light chesnut', 'dark chestnut' and 'liver chestnut'.

Dun   Body varying from a cream to a shade of yellow. Usually found with a black mane, tail and points, and with a black line running along the back.

Grey   A coat which has a mixture of grey and black hairs. There are several varieties according to age, season and type – but all are known as 'grey'. A light grey would describe a very white-looking horse or pony.

Piebald   A horse or pony with large irregular patches of black and white on the body and black and white hairs in the mane and tail.

Skewbald   A horse or pony with large irregular patches of white and any other colour except black.

Roan   A difficult colour to describe. Usually a roan appears to be a mixture of chestnut, bay or black with a light grey fleck throughout the coat. There are three types – 'strawberry', 'bay' and 'blue'.

bay

— piebald

What are the names given to the different markings?

Blaze   A broad white mark down the face. This usually spreads over the bones of the nose.

Snip   A white mark between the nostrils.

Star   A white mark on the forehead.

Stripe   A narrow white mark down the face.

White face   Where the colour includes the eyes, nose, part of the muzzle and the forehead.

Wall eye   Where there is a lack of pigment in the iris. This gives a white or a bluish-white appearance.

blaze   star   stripe   white face

Stocking   A white leg which reaches up as far as the knee or hock.

Sock   Involves the fetlock and part of the region near to the cannon.

White fetlock, white coronet or white pastern   Describes a particular part of a leg.

stocking   sock   fetlock   pastern   coronet

Looking after a horse or pony

What is a stable-kept pony?
Unlike the grass-kept pony, who will be living out throughout the year, the stable-kept animal is kept in though preferably allowed some grazing each day.

The constant attention to the cleanliness of the stable and its surrounds are only part of the work a stable-kept pony demands. He requires feeding at regular times, plenty of fresh water, a thorough grooming each day, a planned work programme, daily 'mucking out' and a clean and dry bed each night.

One advantage a stable-kept pony has over a grass-kept pony is that he will always be to hand when you decide to ride, exercise or school. He will never present the problem of first having to be caught!

What is meant by a 'grass-kept pony'?

This expression means, in simple terms, that the pony is kept at grass all the time and is not brought in to a stable at night, or when the weather becomes wet or cold.

There are a great number of advantages in having a grass-kept pony, especially a pony who will come to hand when called! Ponies living in this way enjoy a more natural environment and will feed from grass which is their natural food. They will also be able to eat as and when they choose and to exercise themselves at will.

But there are some disadvantages. Ponies at grass are not always easy to catch, and fields and paddocks are not easily found! Each day it is necessary for a grass-kept pony to be caught and tied up to a gate, post or tree, since regular examination for injuries and grooming must be carried out. His feet must be picked out and checked for soundness, and at the same time the condition of the shoes must be noted.

In the book *Keeping a Pony at Grass* (published by the British Horse Society) the needs of a pony kept at grass are simply and clearly explained. Among the rules for the grass-kept pony are:

1 Make certain there is always fresh and clean water available.
2 Ensure there is a shelter in the field or paddock.
3 Look the pony over each day.
4 Make a regular inspection of all fences and gates.
5 Clean away and burn all dangerous weeds, etc.
6 Visit the farrier as and when required.
7 See the pony supplements its feed by having hay each day during late autumn and throughout the winter months.
8 If possible, let the pony enjoy a change of grazing.
9 Try to give a pony companionship by having more than one pony in the field.

How much land is required for grazing?

It is not possible to state exactly the area of land that is required, since this depends very largely on the type of land available, the nature of the soil, the drainage and the location. A minimum is usually quoted as 2·5 hectares (one acre) for a small pony, but more than this where a single pony is being kept. The reasons for this are twofold: one, that part of any land must be laid up to enable the grazing to be rested and properly 'dressed' and, two, to ensure the area is not over-grazed. Ponies will only eat the grasses that they enjoy. They would go without rather than eat the rank, tufty type of grass that will grow around their droppings.

The removal of droppings by shovel and wheelbarrow is one of the best methods of keeping the grazing in good shape. This is something that must be done regularly, preferably every few days.

An ideal arrangement is when you can have other animals grazing over the land that is being rested. Cattle will enjoy the longer, rough grass that ponies have refused. In this way the land can be kept fresher and more evenly-grazed.

Can the condition of land be improved?

When one talks of the condition of land one must always think of the problem of drainage. On much of land which has a sandy or chalky soil this is not such a major problem. But when the grazing land is on clay good drainage is essential for good pasture.

If the land is really poor it is better to have it ploughed up and completely re-seeded. The mixture of seed will be important and advice should be taken from local farmers or from the seedsman. The selection of the best seed varies according to the soil, but it should include a mixture of grasses and clover with some of the herbs ponies enjoy.

The addition of lime and phosphates to the soil will also help towards improving the grazing, as will the occasional use of a harrow and roller.

The improvement of land demands a certain scientific knowledge of the problems involved. As with many of the difficulties faced when owning or caring for horses and ponies, always talk to those with experience and seek the advice of specialists.

What is the best form of fencing?

A post and rail fence is perhaps the best of all artificial types of fencing. This should be erected to a height which will prevent a horse or pony from jumping out of the field. Among alternatives are electric fences (these are not recommended, except when reducing the area being used for grazing) and the fencing which uses wire.

When wire is used there is a danger in this becoming broken and rusty. The upright posts to which the wires are attached can also become loose in the ground — sometimes because horses and ponies will use them to rub up against.

Barbed wire as a means of fencing is to be avoided.

The most natural fence is that formed by hedges and banks. Again, these require frequent attention to see that gaps are not appearing.

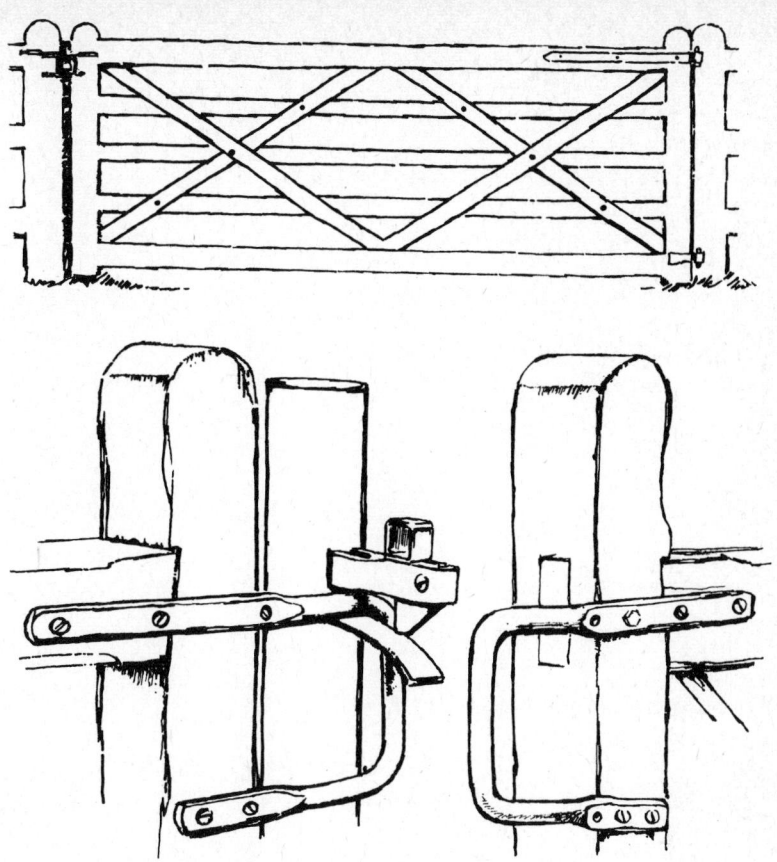

What is the best type of gate?
A gate to a field or paddock must have two qualities: it must be strong and easy to open, yet it must be simple to close and secure. A gate should also be wide enough to permit a horse-box or tractor to get in and out of the field.

Gates made from wood or from metal should be hung on strong upright posts. Be sure the fastening is such that the gate is secure when shut.

If you feel it necessary to lock a gate a chain with a padlock is perhaps the best method. Making gates too secure can be quite a nuisance, especially when they may require opening in a hurry or in the case of an emergency.

The drinking trough is being checked. When the ball-cock is gently pressed, the flow of fresh water can be seen to be refilling the trough freely.

Is running water essential?

The best possible supply of water in a field used for grazing is a running stream or pond, but not a pond that is silted or stagnant. Should neither of these be available the best alternative is to have water brought to the field through pipes.

This will mean having a trough, similar to the one illustrated. As ponies drink the level of water lowers and the ball-cock (which regulates the fresh water coming into the trough) opens, allowing water to flow through to re-fill the trough.

If a trough is in use a regular inspection is necessary to see that it is flowing freely and not flooding. The trough must be thoroughly cleaned out and scrubbed each month.

Static water, that is water kept in an old bath or other container, can be dangerous to the health of a pony. Unless there is a regulator or ball-cock fitted to the supply it is far better to bring fresh water in buckets. These should be re-filled twice a day and must be place on level ground to avoid them being easily knocked over.

In winter months the troughs or buckets must be looked at quite frequently to see that ice has not formed which will prevent a pony from getting his essential drink.

Which form of shelter is best?

There are really two types of shelter, the natural protection which comes from trees and hedgerows and the man-made shelter which looks like an open-fronted stable. Both are essential to the well-being of horses and ponies which are grazed for long periods.

In summer months the horses and ponies will shelter to escape from flies and heat, and if they can do this inside a wooden shelter so much the better. In winter months this shelter will then give protection from winds and rain.

We picture the ideal type of shelter. It should be placed in the corner of a field, preferably with its back to the prevailing winds. Trees and stout hedges also give protection, but these are not always effective in winter months when the leaves have fallen and the hedges are not as thick as they are in summer.

Which trees and hedge plants are dangerous to ponies?

Yew and laburnum are the most dangerous trees and even the dead and half-dead branches when eaten can quickly poison a pony. Oaks are also to be avoided, since acorns eaten in excess can cause death. One must also do everything to keep ponies from laurel, privet, acacia or rhododendron hedges.

Most poisonous plants will only affect the pony's health when eaten to excess. But it is far better to avoid the problem which might arise by removing from the fields and hedgerows all plants, hedge plants and trees which are dangerous.

Never take a chance with a pony's health – especially if trouble can be prevented by continual and thorough inspection.

laburnum

yew

oak

laurel

privet

rhododendron

false acacia (robinia)

59

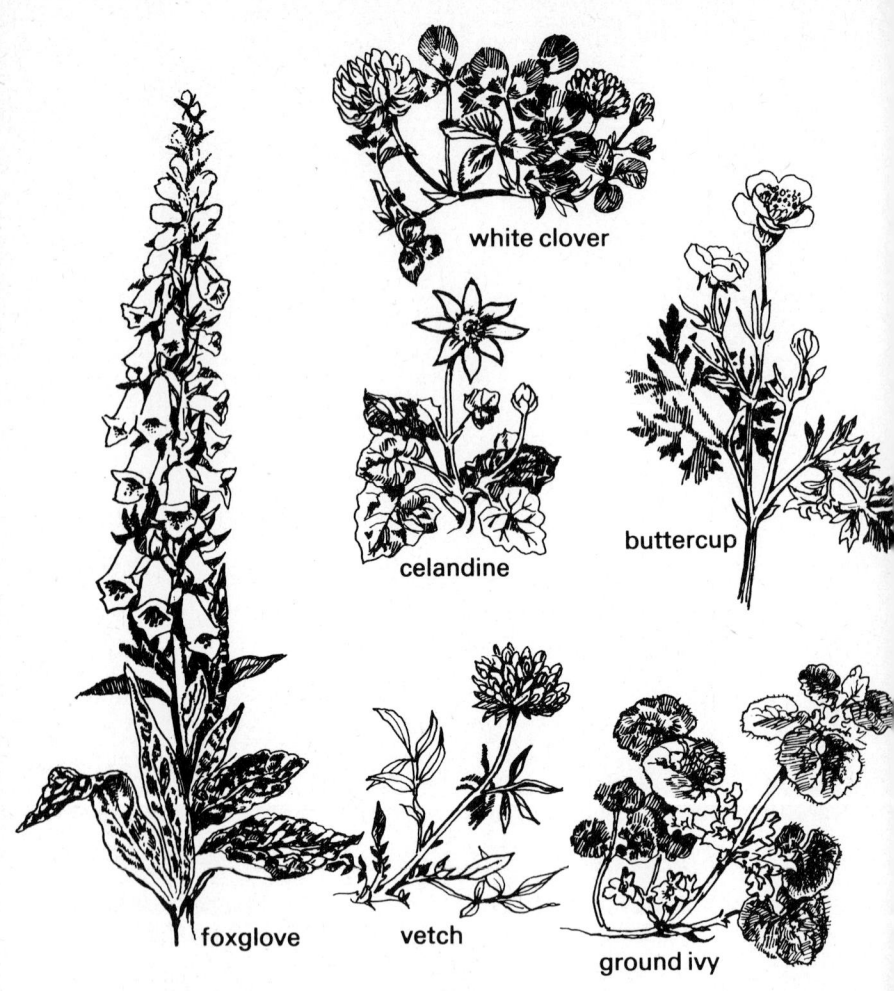

white clover

celandine

buttercup

foxglove

vetch

ground ivy

Which plants are dangerous to ponies?

Some of the most dangerous plants are illustrated here. Where these appear on the land it is best if they are dug up, taken from the field, and put on a fire. It is not a good idea to pull the tops off – it is far better to get rid of the roots as well!

Fields need regular and thorough inspection especially between spring and early autumn.

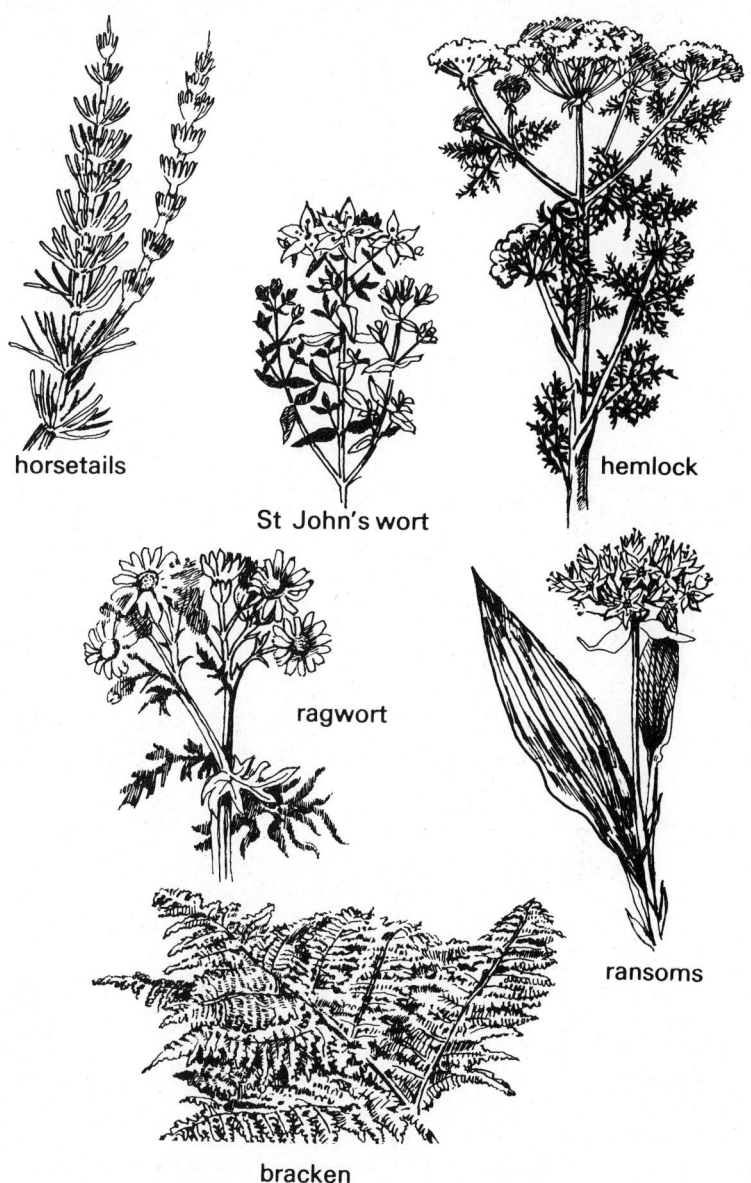

horsetails

St John's wort

hemlock

ragwort

ransoms

bracken

Why cleanliness?

The most important rule to be observed by all who own or look after horses or ponies is to ensure cleanliness. Paddocks and fields must be attended to and, as far as stable-kept horses are concerned, cleanliness has to be ensured at all times both in the stable and around the stable area.

At regular periods the entire stable must be cleaned out and the floor and walls brushed and hosed. Then, when the floor is completely dry, the bedding can be put back. It is also important that the manger and other feeding utensils are cleaned each day.

The area surrounding a stable should be more than tidy! Do not allow any dirt or litter to lie about. Without a constant watch that all is clean and tidy there is a risk of disease.

Apart from a clean stable, clean food and water, and a clean and fresh bed, a horse must be kept clean by regular and thorough grooming.

The 'muck heap', too, must be looked at each week. See that this is well sited; neither too far from nor too near the stable. The heap should be removed as often as necessary.

What different materials can be used for bedding?

It is essential to do all you can to provide the best possible bed for your horse or pony. The aim is for a warm and dry bed, and this can always be provided when you regularly carry out the preparation and cleaning of the stable.

The 'mucking out' of a stable, or shelter, is perhaps the most important of all routine stable jobs. It must be done at least once a day and, where a horse or pony is stable-kept, it may have to be carried out each morning and evening.

The different materials which can be used for bedding include:
1 Straw
2 Bracken or peat
3 Wood chips or shavings
4 Sawdust.

Of these, straw is perhaps the most commonly used; the different types of straw and varying lengths to which it has been cut allow you to provide an ideal bed. When mucking out a straw bed a certain amount of the material will be taken away in the wheelbarrow. This should be stacked on the muck heap.

Bracken or peat are not really as suitable, though either can serve the purpose when other materials are not to hand.

Wood chips or wood shavings are used in many stables, sometimes by choice and sometimes when the vet has advised taking a horse which might have slight breathing difficulties off a straw bed.

Whatever material is used be sure to clean it daily. Bedding of straw, bracken, peat, sawdust or shavings can be dusty. Never fork too violently, and when cleaning out a stable and re-making a bed allow any dust to settle before putting your horse or pony back into the stable.

What are the rules of good feeding?

The most natural way for a horse or pony to feed is by grazing, though with the changing seasons and different climatic conditions, the goodness in grass will vary from very rich to extremely poor. Therefore, when a pony is asked to work, some supplementary feeding is necessary and the nature of such supplementary feeding depends (a) on the nature and extent of the work being asked for, and (b) on the pony's age, condition and temperament.

To a large extent you will have to judge what your horse or pony requires to keep him well-fed and fit. You will notice by his appearance whether or not his condition is falling off or whether he is putting on too much fat.

The questions which must be answered to determine the amount and type of feed are:

1 What is the nature and amount of work being given?
2 What is the age and size of the horse or pony?
3 What is the condition of the grazing?
4 What is the season? Is it springtime with its lush and some-times too rich grass? Or is it winter with little grass and certainly no nourishment in what there is?

Here are some simple rules towards good feeding practices which have proved invaluable for horse and pony owners. These should be studied and used at all times.

If a pony is stabled or part-stabled:

Rule 1 Feed little and often.

Rule 2 Wherever possible some grazing should take place each day.

Rule 3 Each day give the horse or pony a bulk food, such as hay.

Rule 4 Feed at the same time each day.

Rule 5 Always feed good, clean forage.

Rule 6 Do not make any sudden changes to the type of feed. If a change is to be made introduce it gradually.

Rule 7 Never work a horse or pony immediately after a feed.

Rule 8 Water before feeding, but always keep fresh water available in the stable. Allow a horse or pony to drink as it will, whether or not it is having a big or short feed.

Rule 9 Feed according to the work done, but always abide by Rule 3.

How should hay be fed and how much is required?

Wherever possible hay should be given in haynets, suitably filled and hung on a strong fence or at the correct height in the stable. Nets must be fixed quite firmly, and high enough to prevent a pony catching a foot in it after the net is emptied and hanging loose. Except in very severe winter conditions, and when feeding ponies kept at grass, no hay should be spread on the ground. This can only result in most of it being left and wasted.

Three different sizes of haynets can be bought, the largest of which will hold between 4·5 and 6 kg (12 and 14 lb) of hay. A medium-sized net will hold between 3·5 and 4 kg (8 and 9 lb) of hay, and a small net (suitable only for the very smallest of ponies) up to 2 kg (4 lb).

Most ponies are given a medium-sized net, which will mean if being fed twice a day a pony will be taking about 8 kg (18 lb) during

a twenty-four hour period. If we think he will be given this amount each day throughout the winter months we know he will require 8 (the number of kg) × 7 (the number of days in a week) × 26 (the number of weeks in a half year). We now find that the pony will require 1456 kg in that period! And that is not giving him any hay during the other half of the year!!

What is the minimum 'tack' required?

First, you will want a saddle. This is not an easy item to choose if you are new to riding. See your saddler. A general or all-purpose saddle will be the one to look for. Your saddler will most likely have a good range of suitable secondhand saddles for sale and will bring these to you to allow a proper fitting to be made. Never think any saddle will do. A badly fitted saddle will do untold harm to a pony. Fitted to the saddle will be the stirrup leathers and stirrup irons.

Second, we must have a girth which can be made from nylon, leather or webbing. Here again, take advice from your saddler.

Third comes the bridle. A snaffle bridle (see illustration) is usually best for a pony. Reins will also have to be bought and, later, various types of rugs and other miscellaneous tack.

Fourth, you must buy a headcollar — again, it is essential this is chosen to fit the pony.

Finally, you will need a good grooming kit and sufficient cleaning materials. Tack must be cleaned regularly and, while doing this, you can check that all stitching is sound.

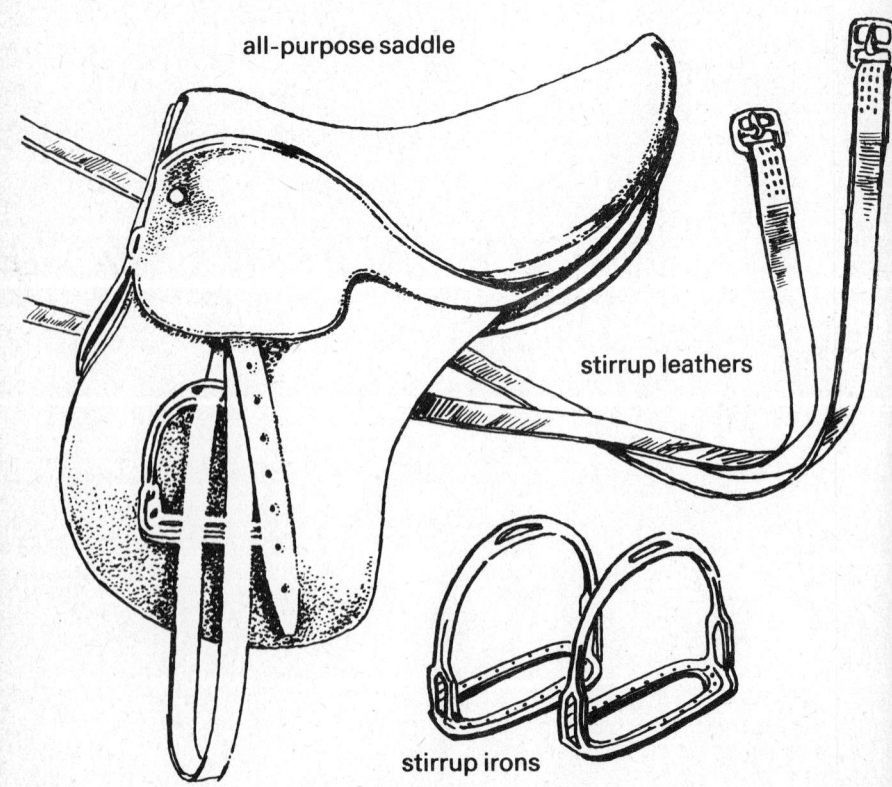

all-purpose saddle

stirrup leathers

stirrup irons

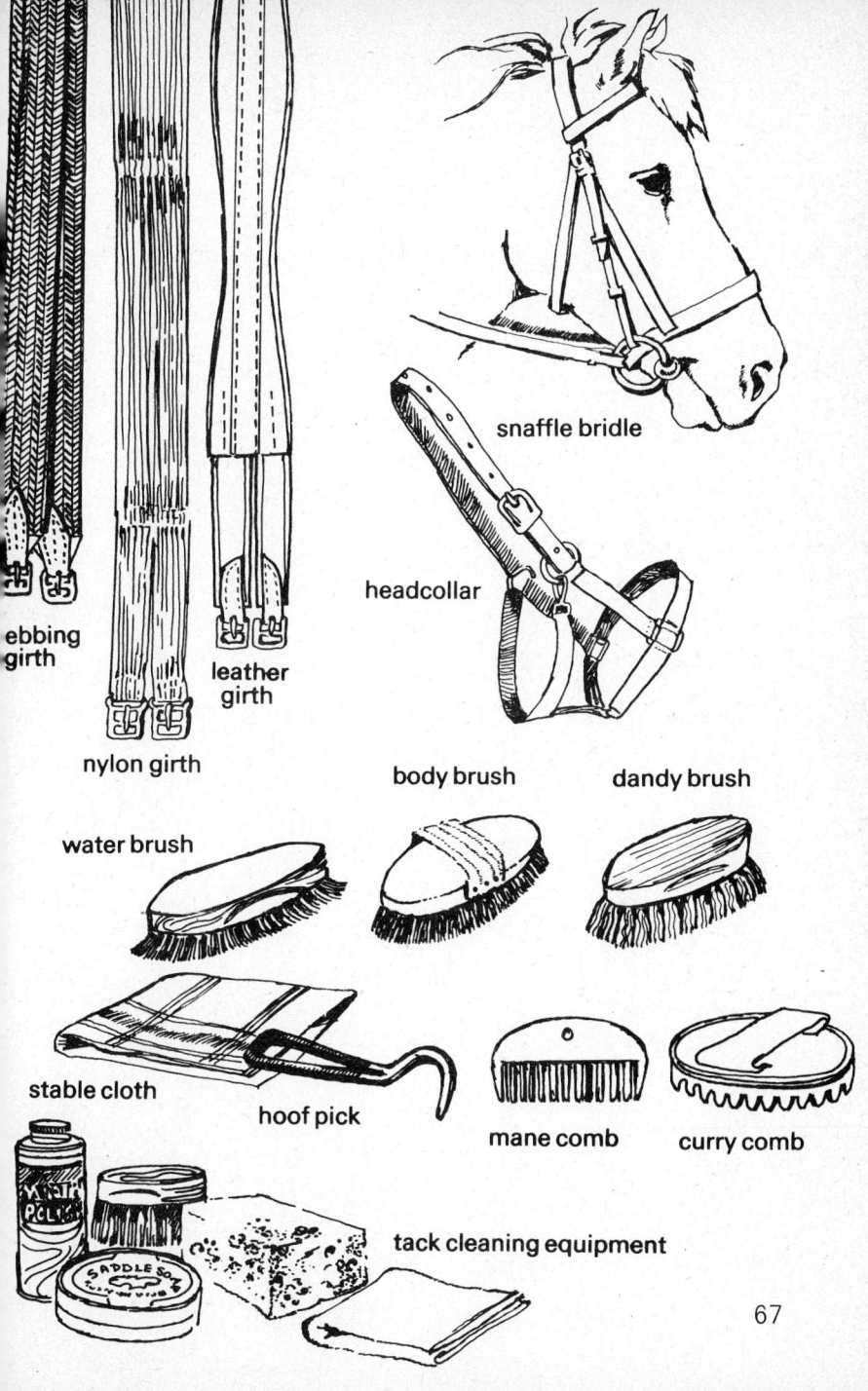

webbing girth

leather girth

nylon girth

snaffle bridle

headcollar

body brush

dandy brush

water brush

stable cloth

hoof pick

mane comb

curry comb

tack cleaning equipment

POLISH

SADDLE SOAP

How can a manège be constructed?

A useful schooling manège, measuring 20 metres by 40 metres, can be prepared in a corner of a field or paddock, where hedges or fencing will give two protective sides. The remaining sides might be closed in by using straw bales or, preferably, post and rail fencing (see below).

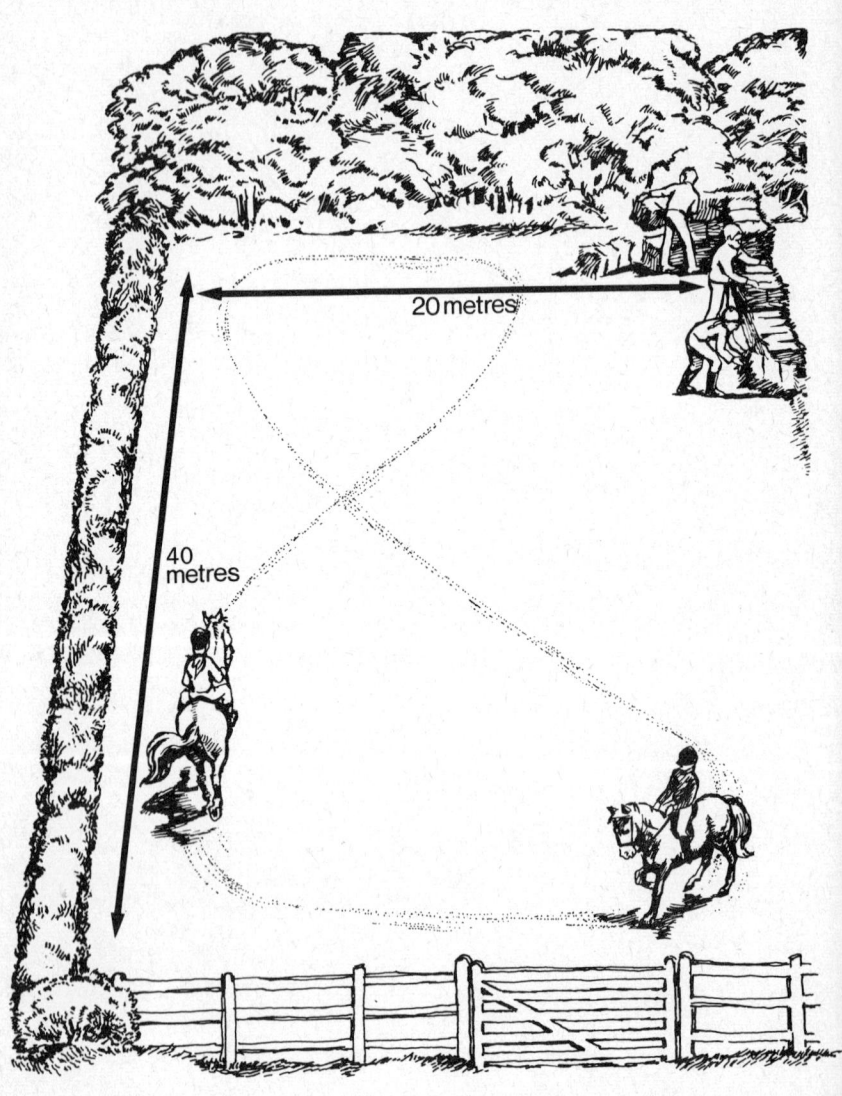

20 metres

40 metres

The ground of the manège must be flat and free from bricks, large stones and other litter. Schooling in this area can take the form of a series of circles, serpentines, figures of eight, straight lines and controlled bends. Each, when properly carried out, will enable both rider and pony to develop balance and confidence. At the same time, schooling allows the rider to apply the natural aids and to learn how well the pony responds.

But do not overdo schooling by constant repetition of the patterns being taken. Vary these as much as possible. Remember, fifteen minutes of schooling correctly and carefully carried out will prove more valuable than hours of going over the same routine. Plan what you are trying to teach each other, and then find the necessary time to go into the manège at least four times a week.

What can be learned at a horse show?

One of the better ways a beginner can learn to judge why certain horses and ponies are preferred to others is to spend time as a spectator at horse shows. Whether an international spectacular or a 'local' show, this is the place where you find a cross-section of the equestrian world.

Classes will be held for the smallest of ridden ponies, and for well-turned out hunters. Others will be competing in the jumping competitions or being shown in 'in-hand' events.

But it is at the showing rings where we can learn the most. Watch, for example, a hunter class being judged – and watch every minute and every horse competing. First, there will be a preliminary round in which the hunters are asked to jump a short course of natural-looking obstacles. After all, hunters must be able to jump! In most cases only those with clear rounds will go through to the final judging stage.

Competitors in a Leading Rein class are asked first to walk round the Judges who stay in the centre of the ring. Note how slackly the leading rein is held.

When the final stage comes to be judged the spectator has much to look at. The hunters, having been brought into the ring, will be told to trot, canter and gallop round on both reins. They will then be brought into the centre of the ring. The order of line-up at this point does not necessarily signify the final placings, though sometimes this is the way they finish up!

The Judge will now ride each hunter, again at all paces, checking for obedience to the aids he gives and noting the willingness and smoothness of the ride. When all horses have been ridden the Judge will carry out an examination. Here he is looking at conformation and other technical detail. Of course, this is done with the saddle removed. After a final canter round the Judge's steward will bring the hunters in again, now placing them in the final order.

Open Mind, a most beautiful four-year-old, standing at 17 hands. Belonging to Mr Douglas Bunn, this Hunter has excellent conformation and has already, at this young age, won many national and international Championships.

While all this is going on the spectator need not have been lazy! From the side of the ring you can make your own judgement and order. Select the type you would like to see as champion, and then ask yourself why it was not chosen by the Judge! Look at the way the horses are turned out when they first come into the ring. Look at their paces and general well-being. Then watch the first line-up, trying to assess why certain hunters are placed higher than others. Watch closely as the Judge rides each hunter. Notice the way he will judge conformation. Try to work out the 'sort' he likes.

Of course, you will be at a disadvantage, for the Judge will have had many years of experience and will have had the opportunity of riding each horse and examining it at close quarters. But you can still have fun trying to match his placings! And you will be learning a great deal at the same time.

What is the Pony Club and what are its objects?

The Pony Club has its headquarters at the National Equestrian Centre, Stoneleigh, Kenilworth, Warwickshire. It was founded in 1929 and is today the largest association of riders in the world.

The Pony Club is represented by over 1500 branches all over the world and has a membership in excess of 100,000.

The objects of the Pony Club are to encourage young people to ride and to learn to enjoy all kinds of sport connected with horses and riding, to provide instruction in riding and horsemanship, to instil in its members the proper care of their animals and to promote the highest ideals of sportsmanship, citizenship and loyalty, thereby cultivating strength of character and self-discipline.

Membership is open to boys and girls up to twenty years of age. Not all of the members own their own ponies, and rallies and other

A sack race is not the easiest of events, especially when you have to hold on to your pony! This young lady, wearing her badge and tie, is enjoying a gymkhana event at a Pony Club show.

events are planned to meet the requirements and enjoyment of the non-pony-owning member.

Working rallies, horseshows, one-day events, inter-Branch activities, filmshows, quizzes and other events are held during the year. In the United Kingdom there are 320 branches of the Pony Club with more than 45,000 members. In countries overseas there are now some 1200 branches with 60,000 members. Young people who wish to join and who would like to wear the PC tie and badge should approach their local branch or write directly to the Headquarters at the address given above.

A yearbook is produced, together with many invaluable books of guidance and instruction.

What is the BHS?

The British Horse Society (BHS) is the responsible body, under the British Equestrian Federation, for equitation and horsemastership, guarding the interests of horses and riders and developing riding for recreation and sport, encouraging the care and welfare of horses and ponies and promoting the interests of horse and pony breeding. It is the parent body of the Pony Club and of all affiliated Riding Clubs, providing instruction for their members in riding and the proper care of animals.

The headquarters of the BHS is at the National Equestrian Centre, Stoneleigh, Kenilworth, Warwickshire.

Apart from its work related to Combined Training, Dressage, Eventing, Combined Driving, the Pony Club, Riding Clubs, and Training and Development, the granting of degrees of approval to Riding Schools, the Society is working to expand and improve riding facilities all over the country with the help of bridleway associations and national organisations concerned with the preservation of the countryside.

A glossary

Aged   A horse aged nine years or over.

Blood horse   Sometimes used for a Thoroughbred.

Brood mare   A female horse used for breeding.

Colt   A young male up to three years of age.

Conformation   The build of a horse or pony.

Cross   A mating between horses of two different breeds.

Dam   Mare, the mother of a foal.

Ewe-neck   A neck which curves inwards from the head to the body.

Filly   A young female up to three years of age.

Foal   A newborn horse. If male it is called a colt foal; if female, a filly foal.

Gelding   A castrated male of any age.

Half-breed   A horse with a purebred sire or dam.

In foal   A pregnant mare. (The period of gestation is usually about 11 months.)

Mare   A female of any age.

Mule   A cross between a donkey stallion and a pony mare.

Near-side   Used to describe the left hand side of a horse or pony when looking towards the head.

Off-side   Used to describe the right hand side of a horse or pony.

Purebred   A horse or pony of recognised breed whose ancestors can be traced through the Breed Stud Book.

Rig   A not perfectly developed or partially castrated male horse.

Sire   Stallion, the father of a foal.

Stallion   A male horse used for breeding.

Stud   A breeding establishment.

Stud Book   The record book of a breed, naming sire and dam of every registered horse or pony.

Stud groom   A senior groom at a stud.

Swan-neck   A neck which curves inwards, but closer to the body than a ewe-neck.

Yearling   A term used throughout the year after birth.

More Beaver Books

We hope you have enjoyed this Beaver Book. Here are some of the other titles:

Ghost Horse Dramatic story about a legendary stallion in the American West, by Joseph E. Chipperfield

The Tail of the Trinosaur Charles Causley's splendidly funny verse story about a prehistoric beast which comes to England from the Amazon jungle, with illustrations by Jill Gardiner

The Glass Knife Gripping and intriguing story about a boy who has been reared to become a human sacrifice. Set in South America before the European discovery of the New World; illustrated by Victor Ambrus

Travel Quiz A brain-teasing quiz book for all the family on all aspects of travel by plane, train and car

My Favourite Horse Stories Dorian Williams has chosen fifteen of his favourite stories and poems about horses; a collection to delight all animal lovers

Beyond the Wide World's End Set in 1810, this is the story of how Timothy, Jane and Brandy the dog journey across Ireland in search of Timothy's dead mother's family; by Meta Mayne Reid

New Beavers are published every month and if you would like the *Beaver Bulletin* – which gives all the details – please send a stamped addressed envelope to:

Beaver Bulletin
The Hamlyn Group
Astronaut House
Feltham
Middlesex TW14 9AR

345033